Customers of our baby boutique are always searching for a great gift to celebrate grandparenthood—and *finally* here it is, thanks to the oh-so-spirited Sandy Shapard! This charming collection of poems is sure to make you grin and giggle, grandparent or not, with its wonderful wit and wisdom. Prepare yourself for page after page of a journey filled with *joy*. This collection will make a cherished gift that can be shared among generations!

—Mary Jo Slidell,
co-owner LuluandAnne.com,
online baby boutique, Bethesda, Maryland

Sandy Shapard is my favorite all-time writer. Her new grandmother book—and I absolutely love her other four poetry books—is my favorite so far. It truly touches my soul, makes me laugh out loud, and hits the nail on the head about grandparenting.

—Patricia Carmody,
Ladue, Missouri

grandmotherhood

· Sandra Gales Shapard ·

grandmotherhood

Poetry
About Life
in the Best
Neighborhood
in the World

TATE PUBLISHING & *Enterprises*

Grandmotherhood
Copyright © 2015 by Sandra Gales Shapard. All rights reserved.

This title is also available as a Tate Out Loud product.
Visit www.tatepublishing.com for more information.

No part of this publication may be reproduced, stored in a retrieval system or transmitted in any way by any means, electronic, mechanical, photocopy, recording or otherwise without the prior permission of the author except as provided by USA copyright law.

This book is a work of fiction. However, several names, descriptions, entities and incidents included in the story are based on the lives of real people.

The opinions expressed by the author are not necessarily those of Tate Publishing, LLC.

Published by Tate Publishing & Enterprises, LLC
127 E. Trade Center Terrace | Mustang, Oklahoma 73064 USA
1.888.361.9473 | www.tatepublishing.com

Tate Publishing is committed to excellence in the publishing industry. The company reflects the philosophy established by the founders, based on Psalm 68:11,
"The Lord gave the word and great was the company of those who published it."

Book design copyright © 2008 by Tate Publishing, LLC.
All rights reserved.

Cover & Interior design by Kellie Southerland
Photographs courtesy of Ericka Croft, Katy Shapard, & Nicole Jacobsen

Published in the United States of America

ISBN: 978-1-68164-674-9
1. Poetry, American, General   2. Poetry: General
08.03.13

Other books by Sandra Shapard:

Woman Sounds

NightFlight 35

Summer Woman

Minor Miracles

Grandmotherhood is dedicated to my six grandchildren
who are my fun-loving inspiration—
Teddy, Tucker, Shapard, Cooper, George, and Sumner.

Acknowledgement

Special thanks to my children—Nicole & Jeff, Nathan & Katy, Ericka & Russell—and to my husband, Eddie. Without them, there would be no grandchildren to inspire this book and to add so much joy to my life.

Contents

·Grandmotherhood·

Fear of Grandmothering
18
Going to Lulu's
20
Grandmotherhood
23
Tiny Package of Perfection
24
aka Lulu
27
Grand Grandmother
28
Joy
31
Baby Begets Baby Begets Baby
33
The Perfect Match
34
Mixed Emotions
36
Jelly Belly
39

Protective Shell

40

The Purist

42

Can't Help Themselves

45

The Complete Cycle

46

• Grandbabyhood •

Affair of the Heart

53

No Songbirds Here

55

Hey, Mr. Magoo, Where'd You Get Those Curls?

58

Eat Your Heart Out, Sarah Bernhardt

60

Our Song

62

My Knight

64

Baby Blues

66

Just Snugglin'

68

Sunshine

70

Falling in Love Again
72
Lucky
74
Babe of the Group
76
Snips and Snails
78
Tough Lovey
82
Sweetness
84
Field of Fun
86
Precious Gift
88
Miniature Tank
90
Gene-y
93
To My Grandsons
96
A Matter of Taste
99

·Sixtyhood·

Sixty's not for Sissies
102

Pure Luck
104

Emerald Coast
107

Women of Summer…continued
109

Bejeweled
112

Fleeting
114

Memory of the Sea
117

A Morning on the Mountain
120

Listen
122

Love in Law
124

Homecoming
126

Those Who Listen
131

Twins
132

The New 60
135

grandmotherhood

Fear of Grandmothering

When I first heard the words
"We're pregnant"
out of the mouth of my daughter,
I thought,
"We?".

But that's another story, another day.

I was elated at the announcement
by my daughter and son-in-law . . .

Then later that night—
in the quiet of our library—
I noticed a photo of my grandmother
on the wall . . .
black dress, heavy stockings,
tie-up healed shoes, gray hair in bun,
again-cool wire-rimmed glasses.
Now *that* is a grandmother—
my only grandmother image.

I can't be a grandmother...
in the pre-bun state I'm in.
Can I?
What grandmotherly image
will my grandchildren have?
Older than the hills... and crotchety,
like the image I carry?

Am I ready for that?

I didn't think so
until I held my first grandchild.
Then I didn't care what image
my future grandchildren would have
of their grandmother...
just as long as they had one.

Going to Lulu's

As I looked around my house,
    noticing the trikes and bikes
    and baby toys,
    highchairs, booster seats,
    baskets of cars, cradle of dolls,
    and a bedroom converted into a nursery,
I laughed at how quickly and joyfully
I've turned my adult house back thirty years
    to when the central focus was babies.
Granted, I love my adult house—
but in a ten-minute exercise,
I can convert it into a
    child-friendly home....
        Steuben up, plants up, breakables up,
            toys down ...
                an easy do.

I want it to be a Grandmother House
    that opens arms to grandchildren
    and welcomes them.

I realized recently that I didn't have a memory
    of my grandmother's home.
I know that sounds odd,
    but she died when I was three or four,
    and all my memories of her
        are tied into her visits to our home.

Still, I am astonished that
I didn't remember my grandmother's house
in the first three or four years of my life.
She always came to our house . . .
    my parent's house . . .
and my father's brothers and their families
    would come to our home to see her
    while she was staying with us.

I have no memory of her being with us
    for Christmas or holidays . . .
and no memory of thinking that was odd.
Of course, I was very young
    and she wasn't exactly
    a cuddling-type of grandmother.

She would appear at our home
    and stay awhile—
    maybe a week or two—
disperse her silver dollars and
then she was gone . . .
    until her next reappearance.

Whenever I've just scraped cookie-dough off
    the cabinets
    or needed a massage after a
    grandbaby visits,
I remind myself that I don't want my
grandchildren
to ever write a poem about *not* knowing
where their Lulu lived.

Grandmotherhood

When Grandchildren enter Grandmotherhood,
They know that fun is in store,
As cookie jars come open,
And rules fly out the door.

There is no ironclad bedtime,
Not in this Grandmotherhood.
We go to sleep when we need to,
Not just when we should.

There are stories, books, and costumes,
Along with paints and projects galore.
Make-believe is every hour, every day,
Superheroes, pirates, and more.

Grandmotherhood is a magical place,
Not measured in blocks or miles,
where Grandchildren are loved unconditionally,
and Grandmothers get smooches and smiles.

Tiny Package of Perfection

To most grandchildren,
    a grandmother is
        a slow mommy.

She moves at a much slower pace than their
    mommy does
        and never hurries
        through stores
        through meals
        through books
        on walks.

She listens to her grandchildren's
        stories
        corny jokes
        epic descriptions of events
        and never answers the phone
        when they are talking.

She fixes pancakes and
> bacon and eggs
>> when it's not even Sunday
>> and sometimes even for supper,
>>> if a grandchild asks.

She never runs out of
> cookies
> nor ice cream
> nor stories.

She knows lots of tales about mommy—
>> or daddy—
> wonderful and exciting stories;
> and she tells her grandchildren often
>> that she thinks they are brilliant
>>> beautiful
>>> comical
>>> talented
>>> perfect
> because that's exactly how she sees them....
>> Perfection in a Tiny Package.

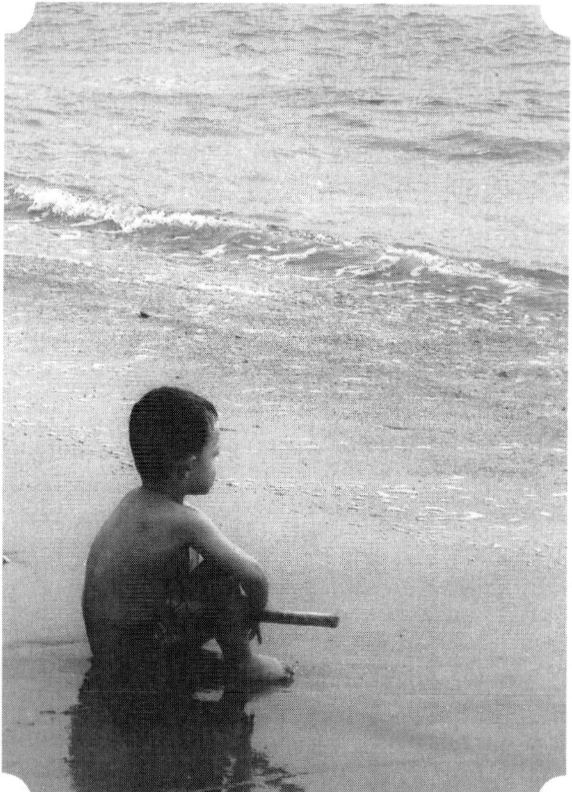

aka Lulu

Grandmother or Grandma,
Grammy or Gram . . .
Nanny or Nanno,
Nanny-Mom or Ma'am.

Goo-Goo or Koo-Koo,
Poppy or Grumps;
The grandchild names the grandparents . . .
whatever name he wants.

So I am your Lulu
for the rest of my life;
even after you're grown
and have taken a wife.

You know that your Lulu
is your puppet on a string;
I would sprint a hundred miles
to hear you call me anything.

Grand Grandmother

By the time I came along,
I had only one living grandmother
    —and no grandfathers—
and she was Grandmother . . .
    not my Grammy, nor Granny,
    certainly not Gram, nor Gran—
She was Grandmother.
And when she came to visit,
    she was escorted into the
    highest chair—
    our toile wingback—
        almost throne-like
        with her sitting in it.

The children greeted her
    one by one,
and I remember her
taking my tiny hands
    and closing them
        over a large coin—
            a silver dollar—
    the same on each visit.

I guess, in retrospect,
she deserved the throne,
>   followed by my mother's place
>   at the dinner table.
After all, she was Old—
she had to be at least sixty
>   —and sixty was the new eighty back then.

She always wore a black dress,
black stockings, black shoes with heels—
>   winter or summer—
her gray hair up,
and either pearls or a brooch,
no rings other than a gold band,
and she always had a handkerchief
>   hidden in a pocket or up a sleeve . . .
>   always.
Was she in a black dress perpetually
because she was still in mourning
for my grandfather—
ten years later—
or because it was the only color
those matronly dresses came in?

Doubtful it was because
black is sleek and slenderizing—
her granny dresses could never fall in the
category of
"Little Black Dress."

In her sixty-plus years,
she had given birth to nine children,
    one stillborn, one who didn't survive
    a horse accident, one who died in adulthood,
    and she had outlived her husband of
        thirty-plus years.
She had known joy and sorrow,
and she had survived . . .
    with an endless supply of silver dollars. . . .
Unquestionably, she deserved the throne.

Joy

Joy has always been one of my favorite words.
    To me, it describes so perfectly
            the height of feeling;
    For me, the word Joy exceeds happiness;
    To me, it is stronger than delight
            and more meaningful than merriment.

Joyful is the best of the best feelings.

Up until 2001, I had held dear
    four days of Great Joy:
        my wedding day and
           the birth days of our three children.

Those days haven't been rivaled until recently:
        by the six days
        when my grandchildren entered
        the world
            and my life.

Each of these six days was unique
>and memorable
>>and Joyful. . . .

And the best part is that, this time around,
I got all of the Joy . . .
>>and none of the labor.

Baby Begets Baby Begets Baby

When your baby has a baby,
All your emotions come alive;
Your baby is painfully suffering
While your grandchild is trying to arrive.

You're in awe at the strength of your baby,
Her bravery brings a tear;
You mask it with anticipation of "new life"
For that's what she needs to hear.

The joy when it finally happens
Is a story yet unwritten;
One look at this minuscule babe
And grandparents are instantly smitten.

Then watching your child look at her child
Is a sight unlike any other;
When your baby has a baby,
Baby transforms into... a mother.

The Perfect Match

We're a perfect match—
    you and your Lulu.

    You love to rock;
    I love to rock you.

    You love music;
    I love to sing to you.

    You love to be held;
    I love to cuddle with you.

    You love to eat;
    I love to feed you.

    You have roly-poly legs;
    I think they're adorable.

    You drool…often;
    I find it charming.

    You have crazy hair;
    My hair is crazier.

You burp like a pro;
I find it healthy.

You laugh; I laugh;
You cry; I comfort.

We will always be a perfect match . . .
                             until you outgrow me.

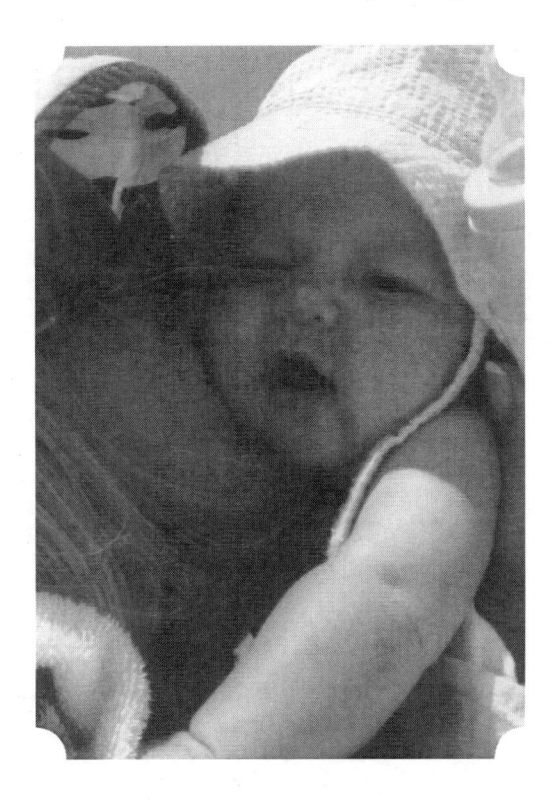

Grandmotherhood

Mixed Emotions

I stood in the baby department of Nordstrom's
    totally paralyzed
    as if my feet
        were stuck on glue.

I don't know how long
    my trance had gone on
    before a saleswoman
        came over and
        placed her hand on my shoulder
            almost hug-like.
As I moved my head
    to look at her
        drops landed on my shoulder
            and on her hand,
    and I realized then
    that my eyes
        were filled with tears
        that had to go somewhere
            when interrupted
            with her "Are you all right?"

My brusque "fine" was followed
by quick embarrassed steps toward
the ladies lounge
to regroup.

I'm sure the kind salesperson
thought I had a sad tale . . .
but it would have sounded trite
to explain
that I was sad
because
it had just hit me
that the week
with my baby granddaughter
alone
would be over that night.

While I was elated
to have been able to spend
this time with her
And elated that my children
could have a vacation
And elated that they entrusted me
with their most precious baby
And elated that nothing bad
happened on my watch

And elated that both the baby
    and the dog
    were healthy for their return . . .

I felt like it was the end
    of a birthday celebration. . . .
        Happy to have been invited . . .
        happy to have partied . . .
            but sad that it was over . . .
                times 4 trillion.

Jelly Belly

No way to explain
    the tearing eyes,
when my baby's flat tummy
    starts expanding in size.

It's not sadness I feel
    about her growing belly;
it's joy on many levels
    that it's not full of jelly.

My baby's having a baby,
    making me a grandmother;
no responsibility, just some spoiling—
    all the fun, without the other.

I'm in the catbird seat;
    observing—in absolute calm—
the metamorphosis of my baby
    into a beautiful mom.

Protective Shell

If I had been consulted . . .

I would have suggested that
    Second Children,
        as well as subsequent siblings,
should be born with Protective Shells—
    little turtles—
to protect them from
    the enthusiastic First Borns
who are too young to know that,
    while the new baby is soft,
he can't be hugged like a
    favorite stuffed animal;
nor do his arms and legs bend
    backwards
like the dolls can. . . .
    A suit of armor
    would be good . . .
but I can't find them in baby stores.

Thank heaven for
>Guardian Angels ...
>>since I wasn't consulted.

The Purist

it was a cold and dreary day . . .
    no walk for us
    no playing in the yard
so, after your nap,
    you crawled up on the bench
    that, when standing up,
    allows you to see out the window
    overlooking your front yard.

i sat on the bench with you . . .
    to keep you from falling
        backwards
    and we watched Old George
        on a cold February afternoon
    raking up the leaves
        slowly . . .
                meticulously . . .
and we both became mesmerized
    by his rhythmic raking motion—
        half-circled movements
           right to left—

every time
over and over . . .
oh, so slowly
until the pile is so big
he brings in the sacks
to bag up the leaves. . . .
then the raking motion starts again
no noisy leaf blower
no team of gardeners
just Old George and his rake
the purist
removing the myriad of leaves
one by one.

it's such a cold, wintery day
that one would think he'd hurry
to finish this outdoor task,
but either arthritis
or patience
or the work ethic
of a perfectionist
make him do his job
at a snail's pace,

which is also the pace
>	and the rhythm
>		that captivates a little girl
>		and her grandmother
>			on the bench
>				in the window
>					upstairs.

Can't Help Themselves

At the Beach this year,
the playing together of four grandchildren,
       of different ages and stages,
   was so harmonious—
       such a joy to watch—
          for parents
          for grandparents
      that even the beachcombers
          couldn't help but smile
          as they passed by
              your sandcastles
              and sand bridges
              and sand ditches
              and 600 beach toys

       and four little Beach Babes
          in sun hats
       slathered head to toe
              twice
       in super-strength sunscreen
       giggling and romping
       in the sugary sand.

The Complete Cycle

Life is
    finally starting to make sense
    as I enter a new phase
        a new decade
    by turning sixty.

My role of wife and mother,
    and all that those roles encompass,
    is spiraling down
        way too rapidly
        way too permanently.

The "children"
    are now adults
    with professions
        spouses
        homes
        children
            of their own.

They now make the arrangements
        of life
        of vacations
        of holidays.

We don't take care of them
        anymore.

Those decades—
   20s, 30s, 40s, 50s—
        are the Real Life Decades.

Before that,
   someone else—my parents—
   took care of me
        financially
        guided me intellectually
        tended to my daily needs.

Then adulthood
   marriage
   children
        became a reality;
   I had nearly four decades
   of being the caretaker . . .
        until sixty.

And now,
>	year by year,
>	I see multiple similarities
>	in my life and
>	>	my grandchildren's lives.

>	We walk at the same speed.
>	We need to take naps.
>	We love foods like pudding and ice cream.
>	We spill things.
>	We trip often.

After sixty, we slowly,
>	but certainly,
>	start to become toddler-ish again.

I guess the upcoming decades
>	will send us back to infancy . . .
>	>	with diapers
>	>	and someone else
>	>	>	caring for our daily needs.

But this time
> it will be our children,
>> instead of our parents,
> taking care of us . . .
>> until the cycle is complete.

grandbabyhood

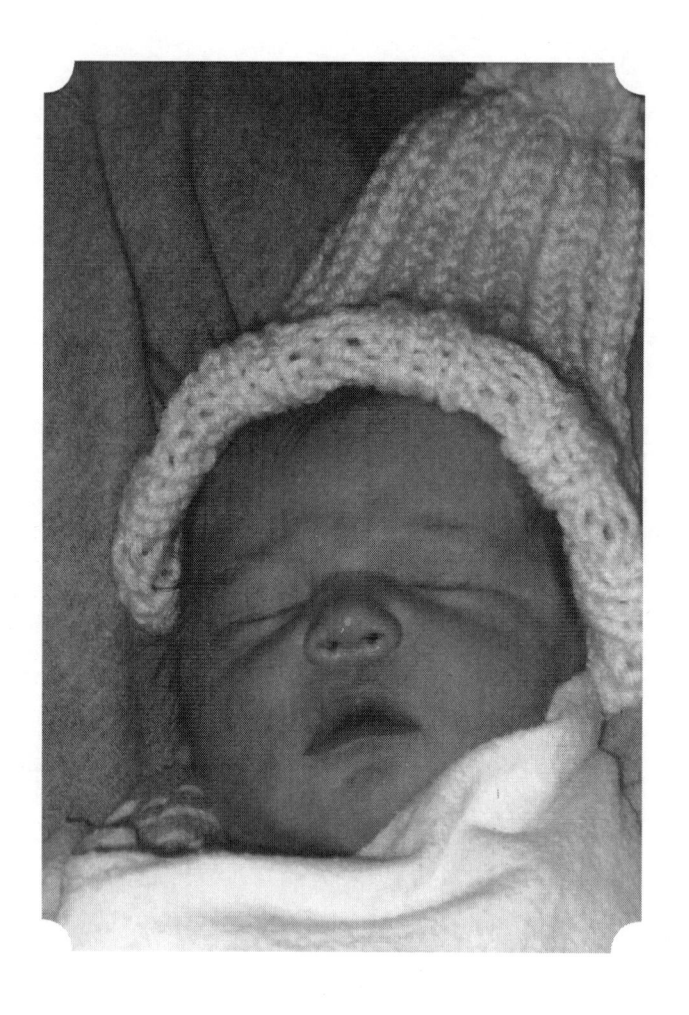

52 • Sandra Gales Shapard

Affair of the Heart

Our love affair began
the first moment I saw you.

> You were wearing a funny hat—
> the kind that is designed
> to keep your head warm . . .
>   not for style.

> But it didn't matter.

> One look at you . . .
> and my heart was totally yours.

Within a few months,
all you had to do was
    smile at me,
and I would turn somersaults
    just to see that smile repeated.

On the days that I was going to see you,
the anticipation made me
    as giddy as a preteen . . .
and I knew that when
I opened the door
    and caught sight of
    your tousled blonde curls
    above cornflower blue eyes . . .
everything else in my life
    became secondary . . .
and I yearned to hold you in my arms.

Finally, your mother
        my daughter
relinquished her son
        for an hour . . .
        or several . . .
and you were hugged and kissed
        and rocked and sung to
        until she returned
to reclaim her baby . . .

    and my grandmother heart—
        that you captured like a gentle pirate—
        could not be completely full again
        . . . until your return.

No Songbirds Here

It's our first time alone . . .
    totally alone . . .
        with your parents out of town.
They've been phoning
    way too often
        for some pretty lame reasons . . .
            just to check up on us.

But we're not talkin' . . .

Your parents are imagining
    all sorts of horrific things . . .
    like . . .
    my not feeding you
        on their schedule
        all the right things,
        or too much.

But we're not talkin' . . .

They're probably thinking that
    I'm not bathing you
        on their schedule
        the right way,
        using the correct
        soaps, lotions, shampoo.

But we're not talkin' . . .

They're surely worried that
    I'm not putting you to bed
        on their schedule
        the right way,
        using their timetable
            for naps and bedtime.

But we're not talkin' . . .

So if we just happen to
>   nap in the hammock
>   on a sunny afternoon . . .
Or suppose we substitute a
>   swim in the pool
>   for a bath in the tub . . .
Or if perchance we
>   treat ourselves to ice cream
>   out on the swing . . .

We won't be talkin' about it
>   because
>   one of us can't talk yet . . .
>   and the other one
>   wants you to stay here again . . .
>   in this lifetime.

So, no songbirds here.

Hey, Mr. Magoo, Where'd You Get Those Curls?

Curly, tousled, blonde hair . . .
    above clear blue eyes with a mischievous twinkle,
    above a grin that lights up a room,
    above a stocky, all-boy body
        with arms that throw everything—
            balls, food, unbreakables, breakables—
        and chunk legs that run everywhere.

You are the first grandchild.

At an all-adult party recently
when Mom or Dad put you down for a moment,
    you couldn't see them—
    all you could see were knees—
then you spotted your Lulu across the room,
    and in my peripheral vision, I saw a cherub
    running my way with arms wide open;
        my heart leapt so hard,
            it nearly landed on the floor,

and I swept you up and got *The Best Hug*,
> with your head tucked down into my shoulder,
and in that isolated moment of time,
you once again reconfirmed—
> corny as it sounds—
that you are the Summertime
> > in my year.

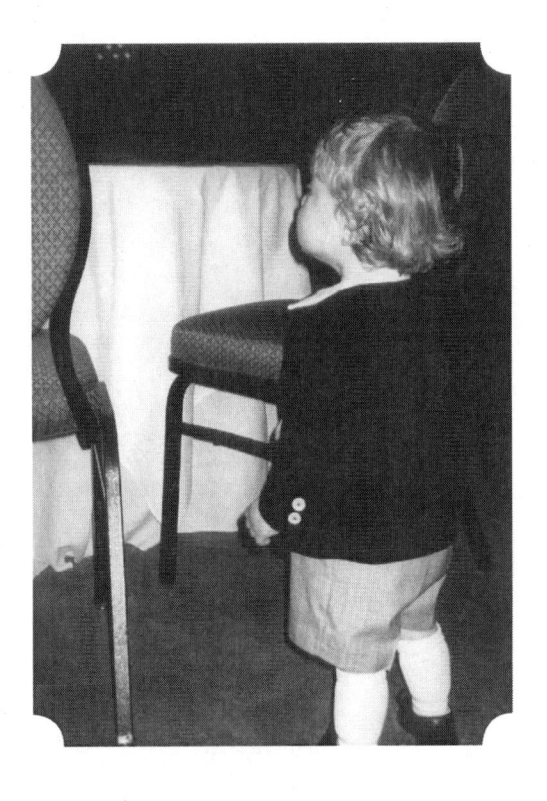

Eat Your Heart Out, Sarah Bernhardt

The multitude of facial expressions
    that you have at seventeen months
could rival any
    of the great actresses
        of the stage.

Your scrunched-up sad face
    brings tears to my eyes;
Your all-face smile
    lights up my day;
Your pouty little mad look
    reminds me of your mom at two;
Your teasing "don't catch me" grin
        makes me laugh out loud
            every time
    as I chase you
        through the house
    to scoop you up
        to kiss your round tummy

and your soft neck
and your tiny toes
   that are already
   up and running
      ready for the next game
      of
         scoop and smooch.

Our Song

Your mommy was feeling a little bit sick,
so I came over to whisk you away
for an adventure and a little dinner . . .
and ice cream to top off the day.

After the long buckling-you-in p r o c e s s ,
we were finally ready to go;
as we started driving down the street . . .
I heard a little voice singing

                            e i e i ooooooo.

I realized that I sang Old McDonald to you
everytime we went for a ride;
but this time *you* started the singing . . .
it was the first time you even tried.

I know what every romantic knows—
a haunting melody is memory's alarm,
and this song will always be our song. . . .
Yes, Old McDonald had a farm.

e i e i oooooo

My Knight

Your golden curls
    above your compact, stocky body
    give you the look
        of a Knight
            in a fairytale land.

You are all boy—
    outrageous noises
    rough 'n tumble
    never a tear
        when you hit the ground—
        unless bones are exposed.

But your total-face smile
        and sparkling eyes
    under those flaxen locks
        give you the look
        of a golden Knight
            riding a white steed
                directly into the heart
                    of your smitten grandmother.

Then one dark day . . .
>   your parents allowed
>   your curls to be cut—
>> the floodgates opened . . .
>>> yours and mine . . .
>   and my precious Knight,
>> my sheared little lamb,
>   was transformed into
>> a little boy.

Baby Blues

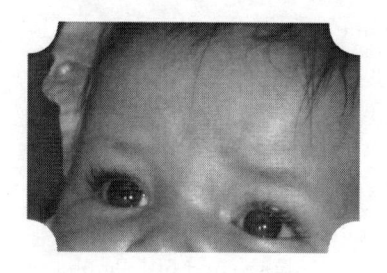

When I am rocking you,
    I watch you
        watch me
        with those
            Big Baby Blues
            and long, full lashes
                that any woman
                would kill for.

When I move my mouth
    to sing to you,
        your mouth mimics
        my motion.
    And when I sing out loud,
    you sing back
        while staring at me
        with those
            unbelievable eyes.

It makes me tear up
>because you are so beautiful
>and so innocent ...
>>just jumping into song
>>as we rock.

I was there when you were born
>and I haven't been able
>>to take my eyes
>>off of your eyes
>>ever since.

As we continue to rock,
>I notice drowsiness
>>finally taking over
>>>and lashes slowly descending
>>>>to cover your Beautiful Baby Blues
>>>>>as you drift off to Baby Dreamland
>>>>>>and I continue to watch you ...
>>>>>>>for hours ...
>>>>>>>your willing captive.

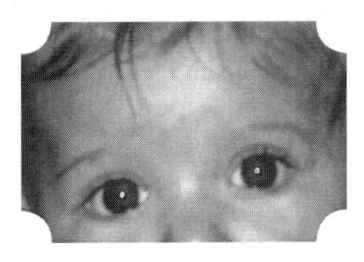

Just Snugglin'

You awaken my heart . . .
    when I enter the nursery
    after hearing gurgling wake-up sounds
        on the monitor.

You look up and smile
    with your entire body
        eyes sparkling
        mouth wide open
        legs up in the air
    all saying—I'm glad to see you,
            happy you are here.

You are totally irresistible. . . .
    I just have to scoop you up
        and hug you
        and kiss your chubby cheeks
            your soft neck
                until you giggle . . .
                    which makes me laugh too.

And the scoop scenario
>   repeats itself over and over
>>   because Mommy and Daddy are on a trip
>>   and we are whiling away the hours
>>>   just snugglin.'

Sunshine

If you're not the sunshine in my life,
then explain to me why
    my face smiles
    my eyes light up
    my entire body
        goes into hug mode
whenever you are in the same room with me.

If you're not the sunshine in my life,
then explain to me why
    you can giggle, a simple act,
    and I want to have
    a movie made about it
because it is the most gleeful sound on earth.

If you're not the sunshine in my life,
then explain to me why
    you can call my name
    and I would hang up on
    George Clooney or Robert Redford
and run to scoop you up in my arms.

If you're not the sunshine in my life,
then explain to me why
    I get teary-eyed
    just watching you sleep,
    and it takes all of my will power
not to kiss your sleeping eyes, your little nose,
your sweet lips, your chubby cheeks.

If you're not the sunshine in my life,
then I can't wait to find out what is.

Falling in Love Again

I didn't plan to fall in love again ...

    I was happy with my life.
    I didn't pursue you.
    I wasn't planning to
        change my life for you ...
        or even my schedule.

But ...
    one day ...
        your entire face smiled at me,
        and
        I was captivated
            by your twinkling eyes
            above that boyish grin.

You turned out to be a Blue-Eyed Bandit
>   who stole my heart...

>> just like your grandfather did
>> 35 years ago
>> just like your mother did
>> 32 years ago
>> just like your uncle did
>> 28 years ago
>> just like your aunt did
>> 26 years ago
> but this time, I have to share you
>> with so many others
>>> who have been drawn into
>>>> your magic circle...by your charms.

Your eyes first attracted me;
your smile then reeled me in;
God help me when you learn to talk...
> and can call my name.

Lucky

You live at the Lucky Baby Lodge.

You are the First . . .

>with two sets of
>fresh green First-Time Grandparents
>>who want only to hold you
>>>rock you
>>>over-toy you
>>>cuddle you
>>>over-clothe you
>>and *never* hear you cry.

We're rookies; be kind to us.

We're setting all sorts of bad precedents
>by making everything
>>such an occasion . . .

Your Birth
Your Christening
Your first Sit-Up
Your first Spit-Up
Your first Tooth
Your first Babbling Word ...
but wait ... so are your parents ...
and your aunts and your uncles.

Let's just hope you won't remember this ...
and blab to your future siblings
and cousins ...
about your Life at Lucky Baby Lodge.

Grandmotherhood

Babe of the Group

This Summer,
    you have the distinction
    of being the
        youngest grandchild—
            on your father's side
            of the family. . . .
        The baby of The Four
        at our Beach Week.

By next Summer,
    Time and Circumstance
        may place you on a
        different rung of the ladder.
But this trip,
    you are the Baby of the Group . . .
    and play with your girl cousin—
        two months your senior—
    who verbally waxes you . . .
    while you physically flatten her.

Play is different with your two boy cousins—
    ages two and four—
  who take it easy on you
  because you are the youngest . . .
    good hearts, those two . . .
  yet when they accidentally tackle you,
    you don't cry—
  instead, you laugh and continue
  to play with them.
Somehow you already understand
  that crying brings mommies
  who break up the party.

I don't know if you have a low pain threshold
  or if you've been building up strength
    for the annual beach trip
  or if you are just Wise
    beyond your year.

Snips and Snails

My favorite time with you
    is when you are
        just a little bit ornery . . .
you give me that little smirky smile,
    and your eyes sparkle
        with eyebrows down
    in a way that says
    "I'm a little bit tired
    and a little bit hungry
    but I've just arrived
    and want to tear into the toy-chest
    and show you all of my new tricks
    so don't have an agenda
        for me . . ."

Then . . .
>   you do the cutest tricks
>   like pulling up
>   and cleaning off all of my tables . . .
>   you prefer an austere, minimalistic decor,
>   no doubt,
>   or you toss the ceramic apples
>   to see if they bounce . . .
>   always turning to me
>   with that smile
>   and those eyes
>   that make me laugh
>   no matter what you have
>   destroyed.

My second favorite time with you
>   is when you have
>   worn yourself out . . .
>   and you snuggle with me
>   in the rocking chair
>   and you welcome your bottle
>   and caress your blankee
>   and you fall asleep on my chest

so deeply
    that you don't move
    when the clock chimes
    or the TV blares
    or when your parents
        open the front door
            and enter the room laughing
                from their evening out
then smile with adoring smiles
    as they see you
    cuddled into your Lulu
    sound asleep
    looking so cherub-like—
making them forget all about
    your antics of the day—
seeing only a peaceful, angelic babe
who is perfect in their eyes . . .
                and mine.

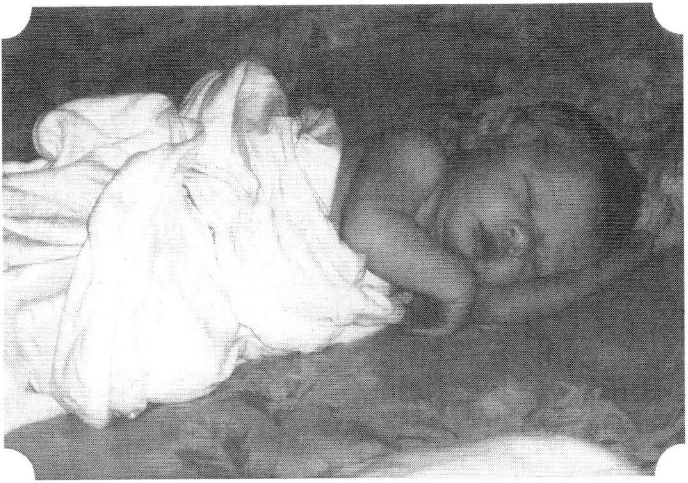

Tough Lovey

You are the antithesis
    of your three years:
        your strength is legendary
        your spirit is boundless
        your smile is disarming.

The world expects you:
    to be older
    than three;
    to be more mature
    at three;
    to be more verbal
    at three;
    all due to your size and sturdiness.

Only the Inner Circle:
    sees your sweetness
    your caring nature
    your feelings on your sleeve.

Expectations for you are already enormous;
>   your potential is unlimited,
>   if you stay on course,
> but, oh sweetie pie,
> can I please remind the world
> that you are three ...
>   and still in need of
>   hugs and smooches and
>   a blankee.

Sweetness

I love sweets,
    so it's only natural
        that I'd call you my Sugar.

You are my first granddaughter . . .
    and you were just here
        with your incredibly gentle nature . . .
At a mere eight months old, you could reach out
        and touch every flower—real or silk—
            in my house
                with such gentleness . . .

so unlike the Rowdy Boys—
>your three cute-boy-cousins—
>>who grab and squash everything
>>within their reach.

Yet while you have such sweetness,
>you can boogie with the best of them.
>>In fact, your mommy came home early one day
>>and caught us—
>>>you on Lulu's lap
>>>on the piano bench
>>>>pounding out a rockin' tune
>>>>and singing along
>>>>at the top of your
>>>>eight-month-old lungs—
>>>>garbled sounds, but definitely
>>>>in the spirit of boogie-woogie—
>>>>>while bouncing to the beat.
>>You possess a spirited gene unquestionably
>>>passed down
>>>>but hidden
>>>>>under   all   that

sugar.

Grandmotherhood

Field of Fun

Walking up to the field,
    I got a blast of *déjà vu* . . .
        when I saw you
        warming up
            with your team.

Even from this distance,
    I could tell that
        you were having fun
        laughing with your buddies.

I could see your bright smile
  that lights up your face
  and makes your eyes twinkle;
    and I knew you were going to have a good game
    because you were relaxed
        and enjoying the pre-game festivities
            on the Kindergarten Field.

My wish for you is that,
  ten years down the road,
      you and your buddies—
      100 pounds heavier and
      a foot taller—
    are still having fun on the field,
      and you haven't lost
        that smile that lights up your face
        and the great twinkle in your eyes . . .
          and I am able to be there to see it.

Precious Gift

If you only knew
> what a bright future
>> is yours,
> you'd smile all of the time.
>> Oh wait, you do.

If you only knew
> that your possibilities
>> are boundless,
> you'd be happy all of the time.
>> Oh wait, you are.

If you only knew
> how loved and cherished
>> you are,
> you'd hug all of the time.
>> Oh wait, you do.

If you only knew
>how beautiful and graceful
>>you've become,
>you'd be confident all of the time.
>>Oh wait, you are.

If you only knew
>what a precious gift
>>you are,
>you'd snuggle a lot with Lulu.
>>Oh wait, you do.
>>>Thank God.

Miniature Tank

As I sit with your mother
    at our outdoor lunch table
and watch you run
    up and down the hill
    up and down
    down and up
        with your brother
I can visualize you
    at sixteen
    instead of two
    looking exactly the same
        as a teenager
    as you do now
        (just enlarged).

You are a Baby Tank...
    an adorable bundle of stockiness
        with ear-to-ear grins
        that don't match the body style
    in your jeans and polo shirt
        and tennis shoes

destined for a career
> as a guard in football
> or a middleweight wrestler
> or, if your Baltimore uncle has a say,
> the first Oklahoma
> all-state lacrosse player.

You could defy
> your natural build,
> of course,
> since you were also blessed
> > with super-smart parents . . .

You could be a superior student
> not interested in sports
> at all.

But then I watch you
> and your brother
run up and down the hill
> up and down
> up and down
> down and up
> > four more times
and I would have no hesitation

putting my money
on that little tank body
ending up as a star
on a sports field
    of some kind
        down the road.

Gene-y

Although we needed it,
  the presence of grandchildren
    prompted our getting
      a strong, new deck
        with a sturdy gate
          with a childproof lock
            to prevent them
              from heading down
                to the lake
                  without our knowledge.

I felt so secure . . .
  for about twelve seconds . . .
      until our two-year-old grandson
      toddled over and opened the gate
         (yes, the sturdy gate with
         the ironclad lock)
      faster than I could.

That's when I realized
    that he had inherited that "special" gene;
    the same one that allowed his father—
    my son—
            to figure out locks and gates
                safes and doors,
        to be able to climb trees and walls
            fences and door-jams,
    all that were, supposedly, off-limits.

This power to enter and exit
    anyplace he wanted . . .
    this dubious talent . . .
        has been passed down
        to his own son.

I'm sorry that my dear daughter-in-law
    will have the majority of his Houdini tricks
    on her watch—
    she doesn't deserve it—
        but she certainly needs to be on
        her toes . . . 24/7.

Take it from the toe-dancer . . .
            who remembers.

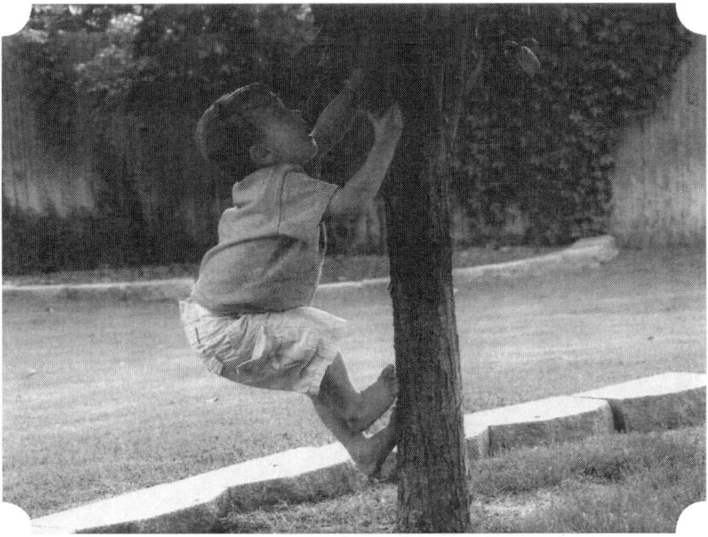

To My Grandsons

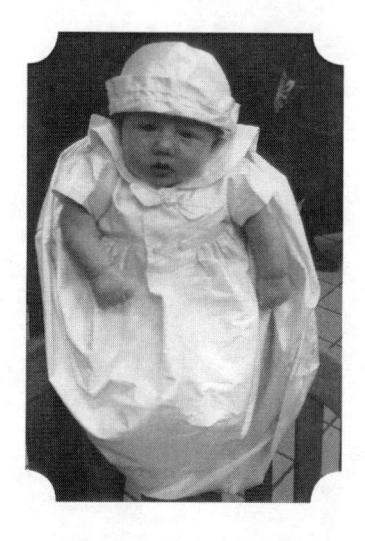

You may grow up to be handsome,
You may grow up to be tall;
You may grow up to be athletic,
adept with racquet, bat, or ball.

You may grow up to be brilliant,
You may grow up to be cool,
You may graduate with top honors
from the finest Ivy League school.

Sandra Gales Shapard

You may grow up to play football,
Quarterback, Receiver, or Guard,
No matter how big nor how famous,
don't forget I hold a Trump Card.

I was there when you were tiny,
I rocked you when you were small,
I changed your diaper when you were fussy,
and kissed your boo-boo after a fall.

I was there for each of your baptisms,
You wore the family christening gown,
You all were precious and respectful
at the church service in my hometown.

The Trump Card I carry is powerful,
And fun to hold, I must confess.
If you ever get too big for your breeches,
just remember, I saw you in a dress . . .

and have photos.

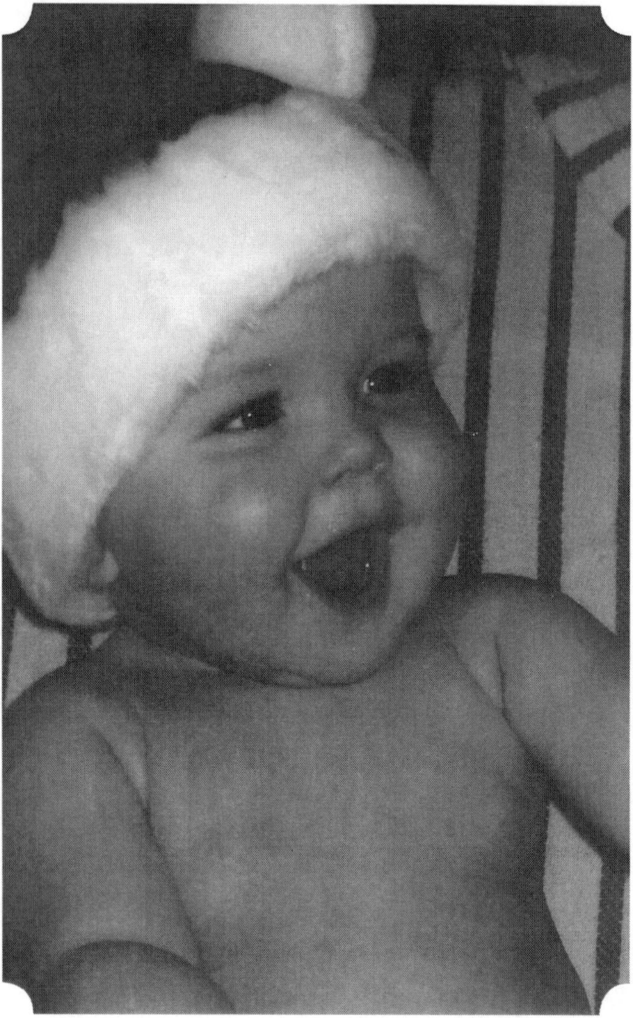

A Matter of Taste

My little guy and I . . .
> we sing all day.

I sing words . . .
> and you sing loud goober sounds back to me
>> that are hilarious
>>> and make me laugh out loud.

You slobber and spit-up
> and walk like a drunken sailor . . .
and I find you absolutely adorable!

My taste in men has definitely changed.

Sixtyhood

Sixty's Not for Sissies

Sixty is definitely not for Sissies . . .

It comes with some heavy baggage—
  The Ugly Suitcases are filled with
    • aches in a lot of weird places;
    • every piece of cheesecake going directly to
      my abdomen;
    • forgetting good friends' names when an
      introduction is in order;
    • dealing with glasses—
      sitting on them, dropping them,
      needing them.

But the Beautiful Burberry Tote bags are full of
- children's weddings;
- grandbabies;
- friends who understand me and can't remember my name either;
- ditching obligation events;
- attending just-for-fun events;
- spending more time at the beach;
- not caring what strangers think . . .

and genuinely appreciating waking up each day
in spite of the aches
in a lot of weird places.

Pure Luck

It's that time in our lives when our friends . . .
    are going through many phases,
    such as looming mortality . . .
        which causes the fearful ones
        to act strangely
        like buying zowie convertibles
        or dating again, though married,
        or spraying paint on one's head
            to hide one's head,
        or going to medical school/law school,
        instead of pre-school where
        they belong,
        or getting everything lifted . . .
        except the
            most important—spirit,
        or starting to talk about
        illnessesssssss.

And I look at you and wonder,
how could I have been so lucky?

My judgment was not that sound
thirty-plus years ago
to take credit for knowing what you'd be like
down the road.
You tell me I look better than ever, and
    your near-blindness aside,
it makes me feel great... and not in any
need of lifting.
You tell me you're glad you married me, and
    your near-senility aside,
it makes me feel great... and not anxious about
your head being turned
by some pretty young thing at the office.
You like our kids and want to be with them, and
    your aversion to aloneness aside,
it makes me feel great... and not hesitant in
having them join us
    anytime, anywhere.

If I met you now . . .
    and had or hadn't been married before
    to another,
    I would think—this is the man I've been
    waiting for my whole life.

    Thank goodness I haven't.

Emerald Coast

On my last evening at the Beach,
I took a walk alone out to the water's edge
    barefoot in my long, flaxen dress
to feel the sugar-white sand
    under my receptive soles
to be joined by the waves
lapping in toward me
    then after splashing my hem
    trying to pull me out with them
      as if by gracious invitation
      followed by a little nudging . . .

    and I sat down
      dress and all
    on the edge
          so that the water
          could reach me
              refresh me
          but not cover me . . .

and I sat like a playful child
>teasing the water ...
and I knew why I couldn't come inside
>on my last night at the Beach.

I knew it would be a year
before I could get back
>to the Beach
>and the waves ... and the wind ...
>and the soft white sand ...
>here where the colors fit me ...
>>the brilliant blues and greens ...
>and where the sounds sing to me
>>as if the water, which holds so much,
>>>feels attuned to me
>>>>also.

I wonder if I could hear its song
>on a daily basis
>>would it sound so sweet
>>or
>>would I miss the space and colors
>>>of the Southwest....
I cannot imagine ever being blasé about the
>Emeralds I see in the water
>>>this evening.

Women of Summer
... continued

We are the Women of Summer
and we are still meeting
   at the Beach . . .
and we are still
   the best of friends . . .
in spite of the differences
   in our lives and in ourselves
     that time and distance
       have created or have accentuated
        when we regroup at the Beach.

The rest of the year
   in our other lives
we have each been wives
   reared children
   nursed parents
   started businesses
   and have experienced the roller coaster ride
   of women who are involved in
     Life.

110 • Sandra Gales Shapard

But when we gather
>   for our week at the Beach,
we can talk out our dilemmas and our dreams,
we have been given the gift of time,
as summer women,
>   to listen to one another
>   to lie on the beach
>   and hear the songs of the waves
>   >   and the sounds of friendship . . .
>   >   >   maturing . . .
as with each year,
>   we laugh more
>   >   eat more
>   >   talk more
>   >   indulge more . . .
>   >   >   we are lighter . . .
>   >   >   and yet deeper . . .
>   >   >   >   as each year's gathering
>   >   >   >   evolves
>   >   >   >   >   into
>   >   >   >   >   a   day   at   the
Beach.

Bejeweled

The age in our lives
  when Anticipation is King
    is a *jeweled period of time*
    that we don't appreciate . . .
      nor treasure sufficiently . . .
        until it is past.

Nature's way of letting us
  have another chance
    is if we have pleased the gods
      by procreating,
        and then we are granted
        the gift of vicarious joy.

That one moment when
    we dream of miracles/take a roll of the dice/
  hope for the elusive/wish upon a star . . .
    is a time of such joyful anticipation
    because we don't know what the future
    will bring
      and haven't had enough past to be tainted.

We dream our dreams
    and sometimes
        we actually realize one or two
or we see the fruition of a dream
        vicariously
    and that same feeling returns . . .
    but this time it is more deeply treasured
        —its rarity appreciated—
    because by now we have had Life
            appraised
        by experts.

Fleeting

My favorite age,
> or time of life,
>> for women
>>> is young motherhood.

I think that mothers
> of young children
> are the most beautiful
>> of all women.

There is something about
> their naturalness
>> no time for primping
> their sense of themselves
>> with bodies in constant flux
> their wonderful glow
>> from chasing toddlers
> their comfortableness
>> with themselves

their casual
>
> attire
>
> hair
>
> make-up
>
>> that lets their inner beauty
>> shine through.

My daughters and my daughter-in-law
> are in that beautiful and alive
>> stage of life
>>> right now.

I love watching them,
> and their friends,
> move about the business of life
>> with babies
>>> and young children.

They aren't aware of
> how lovely they are.

They don't realize that
    they are better looking now
    than they were in high school
               or college
and they need to enjoy these days
               this time . . .
               and take lots of photos
        during   these   beautiful,   fleeting
years.

Memory of the Sea

While I am filled with Joy
    at the glorious sunset
        this evening
            at the Beach,

My heart is twinging
    because it is the last
        for a while . . .
            time is up.

I don't know what it is
    that pulls me here—
        year after year—
    as if a greater force
        keeps trying to remind me
            of where I belong.

It's not that I'm not joyful
    land-locked at home. . . .
    I am . . .
        completely and
        unconditionally.

It's just that when I see
    the silken ivory sand
    leading out to emerald waters,
        I want to engulf it,
        and stroll on it,
        and eat ice cream cones,
        and read,
        and capture its colors
            and its essence
                on paper
                on canvas
                on film.

But when I am home,
    it's impossible to write
        or paint or re-create
            the fresh days
            the sultry smells
            the afternoon thunderstorms
            the slower pace
            the children on the beach
                running or digging
            the relaxed evenings
                on the porch
                after days in the sun.

It can't be bottled and taken home....
>Believe me—
>>I've tried.

A Morning on the Mountain

I spent the morning
    on the terrace in Civita
    observing... unnoticed ...
an elderly man
        professorial in appearance
doing spring planting
        in his courtyard below ...
trekking soil
    to his new rosebushes
spilling it on the courtyard stones
    along the way
then shoveling up the spillage
    into an old bucket
then spilling it from the bucket
    onto the stones
        as he carried it away.

His slow determined pace
    kept my attention
        throughout the morning

as I watched this repetitious scenario
    through the wisteria-laden pergola
sipping my tea
and accomplishing nothing . . .
    but a growing admiration
    for the old man
        and his method . . .
knowing this scene
    must have been reenacted
    Spring after Spring . . .
and his summer garden,
    despite his bungling,
always flourished . . .
    as if to thank him
        for his perseverance.

Listen

Listen to my song, child;
I wrote it just for you.

It's a melody that harmonizes
   with nature's tune.
It can only be sung
   by the heart . . .
   vocal chords are inadequate . . .
   immature for its composition,
It must ring true.
    Outside drums cannot dictate
    but can only be a
        rhythmic background
        for the clear melody.

When you are in touch with your heart,
    you will sing . . .
        and sing . . .
    and then I will know
    that you listened
        and heard the chorus
            and found your voice . . .

and are now composing the next verse
            on your own.

Love In Law

Many of my friends
    merely or barely
        tolerate
            the spouses
            chosen by their children.
It makes me sad for them.

It also makes me feel like Pollyanna
    when I talk about
    my sincere love
        for my sons-in-law
        for my daughter-in-law.

To better explain my feelings
    as simply as I can:

    If I would have met
    my in-law children
        before they met
        my biological children,

I would have fixed them up . . .
>in hopes that
>they would someday
>>fall in love
>>get married
>>and present me with
>>>a flock of
>bright and beautiful grandchildren.

Luckily, the bios and the in-laws found each other on their own . . .

>and I got my flock.

Homecoming

Coming Home....
   It's an overwhelming emotion
   a yearning so deep
     I often forget it's there
     until something triggers it...
        the sight of wisteria
          hanging gracefully
          over a painted fence,
       the odor of cinnamon rolls
         baking in an oven,
     Blue Velvet crackling out
       of a staticky car radio,
    something I can see...
    or smell...or hear...
    that reaches way down
        deep enough
  to remind me that
    a haven
       is a universal need.

For children,
> Coming Home is a direct route—
>> their mother's arms encircling them ...
>>> a warmth unlike any other ... ever ...
>> their own bed
>>> with fresh sheets
>>> a special pillow,
>>> blankee or bear,
>>> their dad lifting them up
>>> and keeping them safe.
For children, home is a place ...
> and the place has the most important people
>> inside of it.

As I have grown older
> and have changed places
>> many times,
> Coming Home has become
>> more abstract
>> more illusive
> It has become more of a feeling
>> than of specific people
>>> because many of them
>>> are now gone.

I had a rush of Homecoming
>	today
> at an unexpected time
> and place . . .
> driving down a highway
>> deep into Alabama
>> after getting off a plane.

I drove around a curve
> expecting more sterile highway
> but entered instead
> a cool, shady, piney-woods
> stretch-of-the-road . . .
>> with yellow jasmine and
>> lavender wisteria and
>> hot-shades-of-pink azaleas
>> lighting up
>>> from the sun, breaking in stripes
>>> through the trees
>>>> as if it were
>>>> reaching out with its brilliance
>>>> —like a blinking neon sign—
>>>> advertising its lushness.

It made me smile somewhere inside
>	and outside

It touched the comfort zone
>> of my soul...
>> just driving along the boulevard
>> with a smile on my face and
>> the knowledge in my heart
>> that some of the home places
>> I have tucked away
>> can be awakened... by
>> rounding a curve...
>> to re-enter a time
>>> when I was full of joy
>>> and energy and
>>> happy anticipation.

It isn't exclusively the
> Home of my childhood
>> anymore
> nor the Home of my marriage.
It can be a tiny pocket of time—
> nostalgic recall—
> when Life was uncomplicated
>> and Love was easy,
>> my environment stimulated me
>> and I laughed with friends...
>> all of the time...
>> and at the same things.

A Joyful Place
    Where the door can be opened
        by memory . . .
mostly in storage but always present . . .
        a Nest-Egg
        of treasure
        in my heart—
        a Homecoming
        without walls.

Those Who Listen

Before I can hear the music . . .
    Before I can appreciate the tone . . .
Before I can enjoy the melody . . .
    I need quiet from the phone.

I need quiet from the doorbell . . .
    and quiet from the TV . . .
No bells, no chimes, no barking dogs . . .
    No radio, no CD.

I need silence from everyday noises . . .
    I need quiet to surround. . . .
If I'm to hear the chords of the trees . . .
    Or a beautiful garden sound.

The symphony of the flower . . .
    The cacophony of the tree . . .
Are there for those who listen . . .
    And I yearn for it to be me.

Twins

My world would be perfect . . .
> if I could be twins.

The disciplined me would be
> an early riser . . .
> and would jog around the lake
>> at sunrise
> followed by several miles
>> on the treadmill
>> while watching the world news.

The other me would
> sleep until noon
> and then watch reruns of Gilmore Girls
>> for fun
> interspersed with trips to the kitchen
>> for exercise.

The disciplined twin would
>> shop at the health food store.
The other me would
>> shop at the mall.

The disciplined me would be
>	a healthy size 6
>>		due to my regular exercise
>>		and excellent cuisine choices.

The other me would
>	eat my weight
>	in pizza and ice cream
>>		and wear elastic-waistband clothes.

The disciplined me would
>	have a closet
>>		full of color-coordinated
>>>			season-coordinated
>>		freshly-cleaned clothes.

The other me
>	is surprised
>>		every time she opens her
>>		overflowing closet
>>>			because she finds an old friend
>>>			from the '70s or '80s.

The disciplined me

Grandmotherhood

>   always has a beautiful dinner
>   on the table at six.
> The other twin
>   gets taken out to eat a lot . . .
>   because it's safer.

> The disciplined twin is the fulfillment
>   of my annual New Year's Resolutions.
> The other twin writes poetry
>   in the hammock.

The New 60

I keep hearing that
>   60 is the new 40 . . .
>> and I like what I hear.

It makes me feel spirited, energetic, and
>   quite fashionable.

Forty is good.
I didn't embrace it nearly as well
>   when I was 39 . . .

but at 60, I love the sight and sound of 40.

When my mother was 60,
>   60 was 60.

When my grandmother was 60,
>   60 was 80.

So I am loving this talk about
60 being the new 40.
>   But just between us,
>> the new 40 doesn't have the
>>> *endurance*
>>> of the old 40.

Grandmotherhood · 135